Solitude of Five Black Moons

Solitude of Five Black Moons

by

Aurora Harris

Broadside Press
University of Detroit Mercy Press

Published by Broadside Press and the University of Detroit Mercy Press.

Broadside Press
P.O. Box 02307
Detroit, MI 48202

University of Detroit Mercy Press
4001 W. McNichols
Detroit, MI 48221

Cover photo of the author by Desmond Jones.

Solitude of Five Black Moons
Library of Congress Number: 2011922579
ISBN: 0-940713-21-7

Acknowledgements

This book is dedicated to my father, my mother who passed away on April 5, 2010, and my grandparents; to my niece Linda and grandnephews Donald and Brian. Without their love, strength, and will to survive, as well as the oral histories of our family that journeyed from Tunica County, Mississippi to Ecorse, MI; from Manila, P.I. to Alaska and Detroit, the poems would not have been written. Thanks to the Creator for everything and everyone on both sides of my family who survived through slavery, the Jim Crow South, and the Japanese invasion of the Philippines during WWII. Thanks to Dr. Gloria House, to the many friends, poets, Broadside Press Board members, my partner Desmond Jones, jazz musicians I have performed with and written about, and community activists who continuously express their love, encouragement, and support.

Photos in Gordon Parks's *Half Past Autumn: A Retrospective* (1998, first edition) inspired me to write the four poems, "On Roads of Civilization in a Modern World." They were read at the Detroit Institute of Arts as part of Parks's exhibit in February 1999. "This Poem Has Checkpoints" was written and read in November 2005 as part of Sekou Sundiata's *51st Dream State* residency project at the University of Michigan-Ann Arbor. Sundiata engaged ten poet-activists in Detroit in his exploration of what it means to be a citizen and poet after 9-11, discussing activism, creativity and academia. After a discussion at a venue that I arranged, the poem's title became the title of the poetry reading, *Checkpoint: A Concert of Poets*, which was performed at the Arab American National Museum in Dearborn, MI. After Sundiata passed away, the same poets met again at the museum to read their poems as a tribute to his life and work, February 22, 2007. See www.communityarts.net/readingroom/archivefiles/2007.

The *Jammin' For Justice* poems, "West Bank Wall," "This Is the Least Dirty Water," "I'm Sorry I Can't Talk I'm Occupied At the Moment," and "Through These Old Eyes Paradise and Heaven Were Springtime," were inspired by documentaries about Palestine on www.alternate.focus.org. The poems were read at the Scarab Club in Detroit in April 2009. The poem "Yurugu" was written in March 2009 for Victoria Alexander, a baritone saxophonist who was battling cancer. After Victoria passed away, we recorded the poem for the composition entitled "Yurugu" by Olujimi Tafataona that appears on the compact disc *The Tradition Continues* by In the Tradition Jazz Band (AFJ Music Corporation, 2009). The poem was partly inspired by African mythology and scholar Marimba Ani's book, *Yurugu: An African-Centered Critique of European Cultural Thought and Behavior* (2004).

Table of Contents

We Speak the Same Language

Remember Their Stories

Checkpoints

A Circular Breathing of Sunrise

Foreword

Aurora Harris's poems give voice to those who are marginalized or oppressed, whether in Vietnam, Palestine, Mississippi, or any other place in her global consciousness. She sees the world through the multiplicity of lenses bequeathed by her ancestors, each of whom represents a potent weave of experiences that are worlds apart—Filipino and African American, Catholic and Muslim, colonial elite and Southern sharecropper. Nurtured by all these cultures and histories that constitute her family circle, she writes from a deep capacity for empathy and a longing for justice, two urgent undertones of her work. Evoking the strength of her foremothers, Harris affirms:

> Their lyric of labor
>
> Will to survive
>
> Is a cane, walking stick
>
> They placed in my spine.

Her people's strong will infuses Harris's audacious stance as a poet committed to many causes, local and international. She brooks no false separation between the political and the aesthetic, between the spiritual and the intellectual. The seriousness of her engagement compels the confident, determined cadence of her lines and the clarity of her imagery—of art, music, or intimate relationships. Her deliberate rhythms require us to read slowly, intensely savoring ideas and feelings. They demand we expand our minds' eyes to see what is before us—and within us. "This poem has checkpoints," Harris writes, points at which an inspection or investigation is performed. "Checkpoints," she reminds, "are found / In reflection / In the mirror." In poem after poem, we are richly rewarded for our close attention.

Broadside Press and the University of Detroit Mercy Press are pleased to collaborate in publishing Harris's first full-length manuscript. This work represents the standards and aspirations long established by both presses for the publication of excellent literature which reflects our highest human values.

Gloria House, Ph.D.
Broadside Press
Rosemary Weatherston, Ph.D.
University of Detroit Mercy Press
Detroit
February 2011

We Speak the Same Language

A Question for the Gathering

Who are the
Illuminati
Among
Proud
Followers and
Keepers of
Esoteric secrets
Found in the cries of
Suffering fallen
Leaves
While we stand
In silence
Gobbling
Crumbled
Words
As if they were
Dry biscuits
Released from
Shrapneled
Tins?

Braiding

I remember those Saturdays.
Summer Saturdays sitting on
Front porch stairs
With your shoulders
Clamped between knobby knees and
Skinny thighs while I
Ran that b-i-i-i-i-g black comb
Across your nappy, Afro'd head.

I dragged the comb slowly
Like a student driver making
Zig zags, side streets, and ninety degree
Turns. I would brake for the balls of
Old hair grease and lint.

I remember all of it.
The edge of it
Scratching away the day's events
The grind of summer school essays
And newspaper routes—

All of it.
Dry white and gray
Fluffed up at the roots.
I tried not to snatch
All the way to the end.

And
After washing.
That smell.
That sun melted fragrance of
Sulfur pomade
On the tips of my fingers
On the back of my hand and
Body oil.

The musk that you bought from
Ali's Monkey Boutique on
Woodward and Forest,
The one that came in small
Black capped bottles

It mixed with the scent of
Baby oil and sweat
That ran down my legs and
Pooled at the heels.
That smell. The one that was
Us.

Forehead to crown
Work your way down.
Forehead to crown
Work your way down.

You tanned and turned Black Indian red.
I'd turn Black Asian brown.
You'd grab for the mirror and try to see
Then we'd switch places and
You would do me.

It was our way of weaving
Lives together. Yes.
I remember   braiding.

We Speak the Same Language

We speak the same language.
In a sweat-lined night
I knew I would love you
Maaaan, I felt you quenching the edges of dimensions once parched!
You were fine as jade in a bronze spotlight.

Music was an unrolled scroll of dissonant timing
Long, thick fingers thumping winter breath
The cold footsteps of refinery workers on Schaefer.

You were intimate fingers freeing ivory dreams
The splintering sound of drumsticks breaking
The ambush of notes in your lungs
A circular breathing of sunrise a circular breathing of sunrise
A circular breathing of sunrise a circular breathing of sunrise.

That night we were blown through a splintered reed
After Clarity showed her face
In the impermanence of our embrace
Disappearing.

Disappearing
In the impermanence of our embrace
After Clarity showed her face
That night we were blown through a splintered reed!
A circular breathing of sunrise a circular breathing of sunrise
A circular breathing of sunrise a circular breathing of sunrise.
The ambush of notes in your lungs
The splintering sound of drumsticks breaking.

You were intimate fingers freeing ivory dreams
The cold footsteps of refinery workers on Schaefer.
Long, thick fingers thumping winter breath.
Music was an unrolled scroll of dissonant timing.

You were fine as jade in a bronze spotlight.
Maaaan, I felt you quenching the edges of dimensions once parched!
I knew I would love you!
In a sweat-lined night
We speak the same language!

Description

She was illuminated dreams
Oppressed with flowers.

With hair like the mountains
Snowcapped and dark
Eyes like oceans
Lips like honeycombs
And skin like gold and mother-of-pearl
In a translucent river
She was the solitude of five black moons.

She is black.
Greco black.
Always black
And bright.
A million stars at midnight bright.
But she is invisible.

She is the angel of life
Whispering to me.

Winter

Body purer than a
Language

Snow, a cold sea

Two sacred birds with
Black plumage

Lift up
My eyes

In the air

An atom
Of sky

A celestial globe

Has their own light

It lives and falls

It lives and falls

It lives and falls

Winter

At 5:20 A.M.

The deepest ultramarine blue nightfall
Blankets and fades across the
Land's stillness and
Hush of light rain.

From the echoes of
Cities to trails of wild fern, the
World's madness is rocked asleep
In the arms of Peace, while Dawn's
Hazy light raises pheasant and geese.

She illuminates mushrooms
Scattered gold, white and pink
Open like fans and
Paper umbrellas

August 29, 2009, 5:20 a.m., Idlewild, MI

Remember Their Stories

November 22, 1997

For my family

I stand before you in the nakedness of souls
That died as Black angels
That died as Brown angels
While sun rays collapsed in the sweltering heat of
Blood soaked ditches when the wind slipped a moan
Over the loudness of a silence as horrific as the darkness of
Edvard Munch's *Scream*
Gustav Klimt's *Death and Life*.

I am opening doors of Memory's shadows.

I stand before you
As the blood-clotted mix of
Africans and Filipinos
In the twilight dust of
A carabao's eye in the middle of a cockfight
To the right of Middle Passage
Pulling and pulling tongues through my face from
Los Dias de los Muertos[1]
Araw ng mga Patay[2]
Day of the Dead
That slept in my throat
As a clump of *liberation*—

I speak what was hidden
About rice and *dog eaters*
The *inferior* and *subhuman*[3]
Who were just like
Our Negroes
American newsmen reported.
I stand before you 700 years old now
Two dollars a head
In Manila / on Wall Street

---

1 Spanish for "Days of the Dead"; a holiday in Spanish-speaking countries.
2 Tagalog for "Day of the Dead." Due to Spanish colonization of the Philippines, the holiday is celebrated by Filipinos.
3 See *African-American Soldiers and Filipinos: Racial Imperialism, Jim Crow and Social Relations* by Scot Ngozi-Brown (1997). Note: "Two dollars a head" refers to Spain's selling of the Philippines for $20,000,000 to the United States of America under the Treaty of Paris. This act caused the Philippine-American War / Revolution from 1899-1902.

With feet on plantations of abaca and cotton
And I am Free / Libre / Malaya !
In the mouth of white hot flames
Singing war songs of thatched villages burning
In explosions of landscape that sing the raw pink
Of every whipped back of
Rice-planting hands
Cane-chopping hands
Reaching through red spaces of
Betel nut teeth and

We are Free / Libre / Malaya!
With my *paquet congo*[4]
My great aunt gave me.
Another kind of voodoo
Hoodoo of cultures
Made from asin / atis leaves / and guava
Bigas and cotton / three drops of blood
The foot of a lizard / seven drops of perfume
Three unbraided strands of
The dead heart of hemp that sailed across oceans
To feel the thick pulse of
A Black man's neck—You
Always need protection
When you're mono / bi / or multi anything.

A ghost from the past
Might walk into your
Class and

Attempt to liberate you.

---

4 Paquet Congo: a charm worn around the neck; a small bag containing leaves, herbs, etcetera.
Filipino words: Asin = Salt. Atis leaves from the Atis tree that bears fruit called sweet sop or
sugar apple. It has medicinal purposes. Bigas = Rice. According to historian, William Henry
Scott, there was slavery in the Philippines when it was under Spanish colonizers.

The Universal Transcendence of Pain

glass beads
a disarray of color
tagged   another
third world country.

a piece of cramped
smoke-damaged cave
of the arsonist who has
some control over the flame
that consumes   children.

their breath is a
reincarnation
a phosgene
another noxious gas.

a row of hot   wet   rags
squatting.
a wipe of the brow means
"change" from the
world's pockets.

the phlyctenular eye
bursts at the sight of sunlight
and looks back.

when i receive glass jewelry as gifts
of unknown   growing   alienation
or the organic solidarity
of the leper that stoked
for the clubfoot that blew
for the deaf that sorted
for the cyclops that strung
for the bastard that beat them

my wrists
ankles and
neck
burn from a mistake
and i die in a kerosene lamp
explosion
that has the magnitude of
a dirty bowl of rice
and some days

the apertural eye
is   focused

and i can see that i am
a custom-made
red polka dot
basket
peacock chair
or sand-filled doormat
of faceless   thatchers
that bleed   names
that can be removed
as easily as the
dots
when i take
long, cold water
showers.

Note: This poem concerns child labor in Asian countries, consumerism, and explains why I
stopped working at a large import store. Phlyctenular opthamalia is an inflammation of the
eye caused by disease or parasites. White bumps or blisters form on or near the cornea or
conjunctiva.

Tokyo 1967

Grey eyes cried cool rains
Upon the Tokyo Hilton
And Ginza's bright face.

Two silkworms named Yen
And Dollar spun soft red silk
Kimonos for us.

Not surprised by *White*
Woman with three dark children
No one stares at us.

Enough Jungle Heat
to Make You Want to Pull Your Skin Back

i

The first real
Zip lock bags
I ever saw
Contained the
Bodies of
American
Soldiers.

ii

I've looked at that photo a kazillion times. That
Black and white photo of 1967, where I stood on
A dirt road, somewhere between Quezon City and
Luna, about sixteen hundred kilometers away from Vietnam.
I was a Black Filipino American child who thought the war killed
People like me. Back then I looked like most Asian children:
Two long braids with the skinniest body that only a diet of
Dried fish and rice with a plate of pancit could ever make.
I dreamt that I swam the whole China Sea with a string of
Sampaguitas pinned in my hair. I wanted to give them to our soldiers
When I reached Saigon. But when I arrived, someone shot me
Before I could say: *I live in Detroit.* When I lived to face
My nightmare, I wanted twenty passports hand sewn on all
My dresses, in case recurring dreams made me sleepwalk
By the sea.

iii

The whole place resembled the everything of the senses, left on high
With nowhere to hide. There was enough jungle heat to make you
Want to pull your skin back . . . there's nothing like the thick of
Humidity and green, blood and chlorophyll, mixed to make one of the
Scents of Death that floods burned nostrils. It makes the you not you
And the me not me . . . nothing like waking up and smelling
Jungle flowers, sickeningly sweet, sweet as Grandma's Kool-Aid
Lemonade or jugs of sweet tea when a breeze throws you off guard
Under a decomposing sky. I wanted to wander away from what we
Couldn't dismiss after hearing water being sucked through stems
Until leaves vibrated into a stranger, living denseness.

Enough jungle heat to make you want to pull your skin back from
Rats and bugs, black scorpions and lizards, a puzzle of bones—
You find illuminated meanings for something simple
Like *real nervous* when you're a
Seventeen-year-old point man that suddenly has to shit—

Bullets and strikes
Rounds and vines
Bullets and strikes
Rounds and vines

Here
        We
Go
        Round

The mulberry bush
The mulberry bush
The mulberry bush

Mud and rain
With nowhere to hide
Rain and mud
With nowhere to hide

MINE FIELD

Watcha step mothafucka
Watcha step Watcha step
Watcha step mothafucka
Watcha step

I remember that time Ma was cooking in the kitchen
And she saw a mouse. She screamed so loud the
Streetlights exploded. The street was dark as cobalt but
Not as dark as this . . . . We sat, marched, and crawled
In the belly of Night's night. Vines and leaves blacked
Out the stars. There were no stars. Even the moon packed up
And moved away. They gave us stars to shoot from trenches.
My mother and her scream, village screaming in my dreams . . . .
I can still see faces under the light bulb in the ceiling. Ma
Sweating and fanning, terrified to death . . . but there's nothing

Like the scream of boys charging through the jungle when
The M-16's go off
AAAAAARRRRGGGHHHHHH!!!!!!

Nothing like the scream of every muscle in your body
When you're carrying your weapon and some
Kid from Mississippi with his legs blown off . . . .

Nothing like the scream when you've been
Stabbed by bayonet and the medic's dead beside you
Inside incendiary heat of napalm
Burning
Burning

A village, a jungle, a city of souls
A village, a jungle, a city of souls
Where The Stones and Jimi Hendrix
Gathered shards of sanity
To drop us into nets
Made of guitar strings and feedback
In a sputtering fog of fear forcing the eerie to creep inside you
Till you're too damned scared to swallow. I never sleep.
I'm awake when I am sleeping. I'm point man for the
Team. I shoot baskets from my wheelchair . . . ghosts
Are screaming in the bleachers. I never sleep
Enough
Enough
Jungle
Heat.

Note: Dr. Martin Luther King gave the speech "Beyond Vietnam" on April 4, 1967. I was
in Quezon City in 1967, recovering as a victim of racial violence when Detroit's rebellion /
revolution began in July 1967. Dr. King was assassinated on April 4, 1968. After finding photos
of our trip to the Philippines, I began writing this poem on April 14, 1998 at 11:00 p.m.

Labor

In memory of my grandmothers, great grandmother and great-aunts
from Tunica County, Mississippi and La Union, Philippines

I remember their stories
When I see them
Locked in photographs
Where the will to survive
Shines from five
Brown wrinkled faces—
Women whose bodies
Tirelessly, collectively
Absorbed four hundred
Sixty years of
Women's labor.

To think three awakened to
Cock's crow at Asian dawn
With moon and sun
Clearing stars.

They'd drink their coffee from
War torn tins
Before rolling tobacco for cigars
Before feeding slop to pigs and carabaos
Before bending and bending to plant rice or cane.

See nostrils flaring from
Dung and mud
Their eyes weighing kilos of rice in a
Glance?
One surrendered my mother with meningitis—
They returned her arm pocked by a
Filthy needle.

To think two awakened to cock's crow at
Niggah's dawn, when stars were as big as their
Swollen fists from baking sweet bread
Before standing in fields to strip corn from stalks
Before slicing their fingers on acres of cotton
Before hauling sacks of their days on their backs
After weighing cotton by patting a bag
Before stripping hogs to lay them in salt.

See nostrils flaring from
Sugar Ditch feces, pig blood, and lynchings?
One surrendered my father to hot cotton fields
Before rubbing salt pork on his skin to draw
Red bugs.

To think five women worked so much land—
The cells of their hands fertilizing
A piece of an island
A piece of a country
What they ate.

Their lyric of labor
Will to survive
Is a cane, walking stick
They placed in my spine.

It is the strength of their telling
What Catholic women did on
Philippine islands
What Black women did in
Mississippi before Islam
That makes me strong enough to walk life
Want to be here, to keep passing it on.

Gallery: Exhibition 5

March 22, 2006

I

And
How has she
Articulated her existence?

Let me count the ways

Who and what constructed her
Reality?

Let me count the ways

And for whose
Zone of   Comfort
System of   Oppression
Myth of Pervasive Reason
Does she exist?

Let me count the ways

How has she
De-constructed her
Thoughts her
Mind her
Will her
Actions her
Work her
Speech her
Writing her
Education
Emotions
Body
Soul ?

Let me count the   ways

II

See
In this room

She sits behind closed door
Escaping the cacophony
Of layered realities—she
Escapes from the prison of
Beliefs / language / structures
Dictating the rhythm of
Her existence

See
In this room
She sits behind closed door
Being everywhere and nowhere
Not being but being
The force of herself
Driving self through quicksand
That day that job that week that pain that
Month that year that pill that pill that abuse
That rape that pill that pill

Quicksand sucking energy through
Clogging veins

She says her I-V tube is
Typewriter ribbon

See
Across from her
In that room
She sits behind closed door
Hard as dried seashells
A fossil unearthed
Devoid of emotion
She is emptied beyond zero
With lava stone breasts
Pitted / atrophied / decaying
Mind humph / Mind humph / Mind
Recalling
Why
Un-cried tears
Turned into tumors
On a $50,000 tread-mill
Of corporate   stuff

See
Next to it   there
In that room
She sits behind closed door
Declaring anarchy from her navel
With a tongue a pillar of darkness
Nothing fresh / beautiful / sexy see
The silt of herself
Settling in *that* cradle
Her womb turned dying riverbed caught
Between fracturing hipbones she will
Polish later

See   down there
In that room
She sits behind closed door
On the shore of herself / body
Tight as stocking toe seams
With rubber pushing blood up
She writes she exists as
Knotted tree branch
Tapping ink onto space
Hundred fitty words a minute—
Forty-six pages later   she is

Words / Symbol / Sign

She Is Closed   /   Do Not Enter
She No Longer Needs Permission to
EXIST

On Roads of Civilization in a Modern World
Four Poems Inspired by the Photos of Gordon Parks's Half Past Autumn Retrospective

1
Beggar Woman and Child
Estoril, Portugal

On roads of civilization
in the *modern* world
the chiaroscurist with camera
focuses, captures
luminosities of bones
having relationships with
realities of society's
shadows.

See that woman with baby
Our Lady of Estoril's
rain blue sorrow?
The Madonna with Child?

They've read the Braille
of dust and drops of water
mixed with rainbows splashed
against feet.

They've felt the wine colored
marrow of rejection
pity
condescension.

They've filled their bellies with
the scent of distant cities
entering nostrils from edges of
green seas.

They've gnawed on the dissonance
del desayuno de los ricos
of the breakfast of the rich
pan and *café*, *champagne* and
pescado.[1]

---

1 Spanish: pescado- fish; pan- bread; café- coffee

The chiaroscurist's eye
focuses and captures
shadows and light
sealing poverty in pupils that
beg for relief.

He preserves her image
with hand clasping stones
fingers bent around stones
sealed on her palm
as a mark of
condition
from Angels of Grief.

2
American Gothic

On roads of civilization
in the *modern* world

in a new world dictionary
where g-go-gothic
means uncivilized   barbaric
a style of architecture

this woman   she is a black
straight line of skin
her width is even. she is
balanced from a history of
lynchings, bigotry and banning

she is the backbone of
America
the black bone buttress
the pointed arched eyebrow
over windows, fenestration
dirty water, toilets, desks.

the invisible serifs of racism
etched in her eyes
are made visible by cheekbones' cross
strokes of blackness.

i see gothic as male statue
in the big house telling nation
that our liberty, justice, rights
are equal to the design
of a black woman's chore—that

we have served our flag
by the god of mop and broom—

i mean subliminally
psychologically speaking.

3
Norman Fontenelle Jr.
(Two Low-kus for Amiri Baraka)

On roads of civilization
in the *modern* world

big holes in the wall
with coat balled up as pillow
are doors for Norm's dreams.

even the poorest
black child with rats, peeling paint
will open a book.

4
Ellen Fontenelle's Feet
Sole / Soul Reading

On roads of civilization
in a *modern* world

The lifeline is erased.

I see the soles of this child carrying
America's weight
Of unknown wealth.
Her dark skin is
Covered with dirt.

The crusted deepness of poverty
Crosses in between spaces of
River, horizon—

That black line there is the
Fairy tale, the needle
Pulling outside worlds
As threads connecting
The divided world piercing
Brother's book dreams.

That line, there
Is the ghost finger
Pointing
To jagged mouths laughing
Po po po
Poorer than a pot of
Burnt beans.

And this line
Here
Says her dreams
Are filled with swirling
Water.

Checkpoints

Easy

Extremely easy
for women to become
a piece of property
a voice unheard
a strip of celluloid
on a cutting room floor.

Take my mother.
T.V. needed
a few survivors
of a particular war
and she is lucid
remembers each detail
of hiding in paddies
carpet bombing
traveling at night
with grains of rice
spilling from pockets
and picking them up.

She remembered
a pregnant Filipina
bayoneted with her family
the way they made
a whole village watch
them slice his ears
make him eat his liver . . . he was innocent
accused of spying.

She remembered
one of her cousins
telling her
that one of them
had told him: *I don't want to be here, I have
family too, but we are under orders.*

So T.V. flew
to Detroit and filmed my mother
made her say memories
over and over—
then the nightmares came

with fear for her family
the ones in Manila
who might be killed by
collaborators who survived

and I live with that

her quiet anger
sleepless nights
small frame in darkness
wondering why
the light of the moon
through stained glass window
is on her face
fair olive as settled
as skies that barely weep
until monsoon season.

One year passed
and I inquired
then T.V. called
said they couldn't use it
the footage of Mom.

Maybe it was
because she didn't weep
didn't get hysterical
wasn't *uneducated*
a *typical native*
like us in photos
of *Spanish-American War.*

Or maybe blood ties
and knots and ties
were too high up
or too controversial.

They sent us copy
copyrighted by T.V.

Now I watch
Mamang's face
pour into the room

like a cold milky fog
for insomniac daughters
and I drink each take
without complaint
shot after shot
until the rewind button
makes a dent in my thumb.

So this is how
a mother and
her daughter
tell pieces of history
in a descendant's
truth video made from
poet's
ink.

Note: This poem was written after I received word that ABC News decided not to use my
mother's interview about WWII atrocities for Peter Jennings's 1999 "The Century" Special.

This Poem Has Checkpoints

Main Entry: Check point
Function: *noun*
A point at which an inspection or investigation is performed

This poem is my country.
This poem is all citizens.
This poem has checkpoints.
This poem is equal power, economic resources,
Education and ability to succeed.
This poem is the depth of hate, racism, sexism, and greed
In a room where humanity moves towards
Dialogue and freedom
The freedom to imprint each citizen's life on
Hearts and minds
Where discrimination
Occupation by force
Stereotypes and
Lies are
Exposed to find
What's left of self respect and
Respect of others
Where the source of inhumanity in our souls is
Uncovered
Defined
Drawn from each distorted reality of why we
Dislike or hate each other.

This poem has checkpoints.

Whom does America belong to really?
What color of skin was your last humiliation?
Source of fear?
What white privilege did you exercise today?
How many times were you followed by police?
Did you ask yourself, "Am I a racist?"
Did you ask yourself, "How do I practice racism?"
Did you ask yourself, "How homophobic am I?"
What shade of Sexism is your favorite?
What shade and body type of Racism is your favorite?
What box called home, office, school or club

Do you collectively wear blinders in?
Who did you tease or bully today?
What level of emotional or physical torture
Turns you on?
What have you been told about citizens from other
Cities, countries, religions or towns?
Who did you marginalize or redline today?
What gender bias did you express today?
Whose hand did you refuse to hold?
Whose application did you deny?
What body on streets and in war zones did you
Laugh at   look at   walk over?
How many times a day, week or month do you practice
Peace, non-violence, conflict resolution, compassion?
How do you express it?
When was the last time you offered
A cup of coffee
Tea, small talk
Or recipe to
An African American, a Native American
A Palestinian, a Jew, a Mexican, a Vietnamese
A Catholic, Baptist, Muslim, Buddhist, Hindu?
Where's a safe place you can take them to
Dialogue about peace?
What is an American?
What is your responsibility to most that suffer?

This poem is my country.

Checkpoints are found
In reflection
In the mirror.

When the "Poets" Became Jukeboxes
A Response to Dudley Randall's "A Poet Is Not a Jukebox"

You wrote: "A poet is not a jukebox
So don't tell me what to write."

Well, I apologize, Dudley. I mean
I really feel you, but from my own
Deep bag of surviving and hearing about
Whips cracking, gunfire, kerosene,
Visions of spit and screams,
Burning trees with melting Black flesh,
Bayonets gutting pregnant Filipinas,
Shiny surgical knives in
White physicians' hands slicing
Wombs of un-anesthetized
Black women to advance the
Science of gynecology, and
Experiments that infected Black men
With syphilis cuz Whites believed Blacks
Could not feel pain and were soul-less—

After forty years of poetry
When the "poets" became jukeboxes,
I asked them to write, and I
Had to tell them what to write, and
Teach them how to write, read and spell, and
Move some sense of humanity in them, see?
Get some sense of pride in them, you see?
Get some self-respect, respect for elders,
One another and babies, you see, cuz

When the "poets" became jukeboxes and
Wrote about what they *feel* and set
Pens in motion, their ears were slots where quarters were
Top 10 Clear Channel quarter note bass beat
Repeated raps and they were
Hypno-vized into visions of looking rich
While poor, and their heads became
Downloaded depositories of violence, and
Self-destruction burned on CD's instead of
Wax, and, unlike you, who
Wrote about Love and Consciousness, they

Write to call each other Pimps, Bitches, and
Hos cuz fucking is not equated with
Romantic love, and to gang bang,
Have a train run on a little sistah is a
Normal rite of passage
Where they think they have achieved
Womanhood / Manhood, and
Gangsta Love means you gotta kill some
Body *any* body to fit in.

And when violence, rape, and fucking to feed a need
Became Continuing Education on the streets
        (Love 101 located in the basement of the
        Department of Consumerism), and

Black love grew into a marketable change maker
And babies and babies and babies and babies
Pregnant with babies and babies having babies,

The Black family was built down
Into a reality of scholarly, urban reports
And billions of dollars in sales from
Marginalized "Welfare-State Single-Mothers"
Caught like deer in fluorescent eyes of
Shopping malls or they were
Captured in a room filled with the
Acidic stench of crack and weed smoke.

And then *teenage girls* became *females*
Who were not alone when they
Reclined in the fog and drone
Of pyro-hypnotic beats and latest marketed-to-
Blacks-Only alcoholic drink fads
Blounts and Chronic to escape into a
Sense of wanting to feel wanted and they
Aspired to be video ho's by
Grinding hips out of week-old, grimy, smelly
Jeans hanging below asses, and sliding outta
Borrowed or stolen thongs or G-Strings.

All of this was supposed to be
Black America's fault, but
when the "poets" became jukeboxes,

I asked them to write from photos of burlap
Bags over lynched black faces, the bags of
Knotted, crooked knuckles, and spines of stereotyped
So-called *Animals*, *Barbarians*, and *Primitives* that were
Forced into labor to forge a *"Melting Pot"* that:

    a. Could care less about
        Negroes that hoped
        to be recognized, known or
        identified as plain ol' *American*

    b. Destroyed and subjugated the histories and
        Knowledge of nonwhite people, and

    c. Programmed American youth into thinking
        Killing folks with your skin color is
        Normal, without thinking once

About vocabulary words like:
Slavery, Selma, Segregation, Struggle
Civil Rights, Liberation, Voting
Style, Audience, Theme, Form
Meter or Stanza

When the "poets" became jukeboxes,
When juveniles got sentences called
Life without parole, I showed them
Morgue photos of war, the gun-blasted,
Decomposed faces of youth called
Mules. I asked them to write past the
Shocked, frozen, bulging eyes
That saw death coming.
Write protest poems against
The Dealers, Agents, Hustlers, and
The Recording Industry.
Write against raping and prostituting as
Status symbols and a new definition of
Black Man or *Woman*.

When the "poets" became jukeboxes,
My White, Hispanic, Asian, and Native American
Students replayed personas by acting
"Black" or like Black so-called

Hustlers, Pimps, and Hos cuz
They think everyone in Hip Hop Culture
Acts that way, when they don't and
When the "poets" became jukeboxes,
They called me *Old Skool* and
Too Deep for making them
Think, when 60 percent of my students
Never held a gun, grew up in
Good homes with good
Parents, Siblings, Grandparents
Aunties and Uncles, while the other
40 percent grew up in Halloween orange
County Juvenile Facility jumpsuits
And at the age of 15, were up for
Murder one, and the girls who were left
Were medicated into
Swollen-faced, weeping zombies to
Deal with rape, molestation,
Being sold, and running away.

When the "poets" became jukeboxes,
I read from and gave away copies of your book,
"The Black Poets," while playing Coltrane.
I asked the "poets" to
Write like Etheridge Knight cuz it will save
Your ass and mind in prison.
Write Like Naomi Long Madgett's *Midway* or
Sonia Sanchez's *a chant for young / brothas and sistuhs*
Until your souls get right and
You can lift heavy feet from these dingy
Yellow tiles to walk past cold cell bars
Caked and flaking the dried sweat and tears
Of children's desperate hands and faces

Write 'til you can walk without chains on your ankles.
Write past this hellhole / this stifling / sweltering
Suffocating room of un-brushed teeth, belches, and farts
My Daughters / My Sistuhs / My Sons / My Brothas.
Write like Amiri Baraka's *Numbers / Letters.*
Write past The Empty. The Shallow.
The Mediocre Clichéd Existence.
The split second moment of a thrill.
The description of The Girl as Bitch.

Write past the hollowed-out sense of
Love and reasoning found in
Carolyn M. Rodgers *Now Ain't That Love?*
Write about
How long real love is supposed to last.
What does it look like? Smell like?
Who gives real love? What is self-love?
A Bitch in the dictionary is a
Female dog or a *Malicious Female.*
Who can spell Malicious? What is Malicious?
Look it up. What harm do you intend to do to
Yourself, your family, folks on the street?
Behind steel doors and bars?

When the "poets" became jukeboxes,
Controlled by radio airwaves and gangsta rap videos,
Coltrane's music made
Uncombed heads hurt from real notes
Activating brain cells in polarized
Hemispheres that could only respond to
Bass on high, rattling speakers.

And the brothas screamed:
Shut it off! I'm starting to cycle!

And they began
Nervously bouncing one leg real fast
Rocking or pacing to keep from becoming
Violent and smashing the tape player, and
I asked them to write. I told them the
Headache would not last. I asked them to try
To listen to the way Coltrane wrote poetry
With feeling, spirituality, and moods through music.

When the "poets" became jukeboxes
The "poets" covered their ears and
I shut Coltrane off cuz they began to
Sweat profusely. I saw eyes dart from
Red flashes and blue sparks
Short circuiting brains and confusing
Cells and nerves trying to communicate past

Calcified corpus callosum¹ and I watched them
Spit into each other's faces
Their raps about
Killing each other or fucking hos
And then I told them:

"Hip hop started out as a non-violent
Social movement against gang fighting
In da 'hood, so write a poem about
One Good Thing about yourself or
What We Were Like Before We Became Gangstas"

When the "poets" became jukeboxes,
I played Coltrane's *Favorite Things* to settle
The brothas and asked them to write about
Favorite things they did before
Thug Life. Write
Consciousness-raising poems.
Write a Vision of what a
Healthy family, planet,
Relationship or neighborhood looks like.

What is the opposite of
Bread on shelves eaten by mice,
Slimy green or
Brown meat sold in
Our neighborhood grocery stores?

I apologize, Dudley, but
when the "poets" became jukeboxes,
I asked them to write
Poems like yours and those of
Poets you published.
Break dance words past
Monotonous popular beats of
Self hate, destruction, lies, and violence.
Write like your life
Depended on a metaphor.

After I said all that

---

1 The corpus callosum is a structure of the mammalian brain in the longitudal fissure that connects the left and right cerebral hemispheres.

Most of the jukebox
Self-identified Thugs and Bitches
Broke down, wept, and
Began writing poems about being

Children   again.

West Bank Wall

Four Poems from the "Jammin' for Justice" Poetry Reading

A teacher talks about her homeland—

Along this Wall
And behind this Wall is
Take, take, take
From sunup to sundown
They take
From North to South to East to West
They take.
First they came with blank checks
And when we wouldn't sell our homes
They illegally took our homes and
Land for *security reasons*
And gave them to the
Jewish settlers.
This wall protects illegal settlers.

Our Abu Dis neighbors
In two-hundred-fifty
New housing units of
The Kidmat Zion settlement are
1,500 ideological settlers. They
Take, take, take
Our roads, schools, freedom. Push
All Arabs out.

They took most of the water wells
Set a twenty-seven foot wall between
Them and us where the Holy Land is.
The Holy Basin blocks
Us from everything and anything
Concerning a speck of quality of life.

Take, take, take.
They take our privacy.
They watch us. Every movement on
This road is seen by cameras.
Cameras on the Wall
Point like weapons at
Our kitchens, bedrooms, bathrooms.

Our taxes pay for bodyguards and
Security to protect Jewish lives
And stolen properties that
Belong to us.
Take, take, take
Our taxes don't pay for armies or
Security to protect our families,
My neighbors, and me.

Along this Wall
And behind this Wall is
Take, take, take
From sunup to sundown
They take.

I'm Sorry I Can't Talk
I'm Occupied at the Moment

I'm sorry I can't talk I'm
Occupied at the moment.
Where the days appear Godless
I know God will save us
When our villages and crops are
Burning urns of flesh and bone
Garbage and ashes
Where the *good hours* of
Daylight are reserved for
Them. I'm sorry I'm busy I'm
Occupied at the moment
Where our lives are measured by the
Length of a rifle, a drop of water
The width of a tank
The boom of exploding missiles
Where everyone is a target
Where the bakery can't bake when
There is no water, sugar or flour, and
Particles of dust and shrapnel with
Blood, tears and terror
That we inhale, are mixed with our
Spit to form the bread dough that fills
Our bellies.

I'm sorry I can't talk I'm occupied at
The moment, where the market is
Closed, where there is no meat
Where we gave up farming
Behind the Wall they built
Where our village is a part of their
Firing range for practice
Where the air smells like gunpowder
Where the place where your Jesus
Was born has been blocked as
Arab land
Where the well called Lahai Roi
Where God gave Hagar and Ishmael
Water between Kadesh and Bared has
Been stolen by Israelis to route the
Water to Romanian
Jewish settlers

I'm sorry I'm busy I'm in an
Occupied state where our lives and
Cultural memories are being
Destroyed. Where apartheid, genocide
And oppression are sanctioned
Where every drained well is a
Haunted, ancient flute carrying dull tones
Of buried requiems disrupted.

Sit. Sit. Rest. Sit by this well.
Press your ears against these stones.
Maybe you will hear
The music that accompanies
Starvation, thirst, suffering, death
Tears, wailing, prayers, and cries for
Justice and peace.

This Is the Least Dirty Water

I guess the Green Line
Between Israel and Palestine is like
8 Mile road separating the
Suburban from the Urban.
Like most Black Detroiters
Since 1967
Palestinians have watched
Their lives being eroded by
Invisible and visible forces
Along a timeline of
Spatial desolation and remoteness—
They too, have no access to
Quality food and they pay
A dear price for water like
Over-taxed Detroiters.

When it rains
Palestinians can't collect it.
Palestinian wells are kept
Under Israeli guard, lock
Key and meter
Where Israelis illegally drill for
Water along the Green Line.

In Bardala, Palestinians once had
Twenty-two wells, now they have
Two. Israelis installed pipes and
Control how far into the ground
Palestinians can drill.
Arabs can only touch the surface of the water.
Israelis can drill 400 to 500 feet to get clean water.
They control
All the water.

It's like Oakland and Macomb
Counties wanting to control
Detroit's Water Board and processing plant.

When one settler was killed
The Israelis destroyed most of the
Crops by reducing the water

From 500,000 cubic meters to 400.
In Shuqba Village, surrounded by dry,
Barren, rocky land, water is expensive.
An Arab man said:
One Jew up there has enough water
For an *entire* village while we
Have no water to wash. We take only one
Shower in a fortnight, and water sold
From a tanker is polluted.
1000 cubic meters a day for our village
10,000 cubic meters a day for the Jews.

In another village, down the road
From the Salem Prison Camp
Open sewage flows into
Natural springs but Palestinians still
Drink it.

This is the least dirty water
An elderly man says.

In the occupied land of
Pizgat Zeev
In a refugee settlement, a
        long
        thin
        pipe
        runs
        down
        the
        side
        of
        a
        building
                At the bottom of the pipe
                On the right is a hole where sewage
                And solid shit drain out.

On the left side is a spigot
For the polluted water
They drink. This
Is the least
Dirty water.

Through These Old Eyes
Paradise and Heaven Were Springtime

I pass my days playing backgammon with my friend.
I look across this camp and through these old eyes
I remember this land, between the
Mediterranean Sea and the Jordan River
In 1948, being split by the
British, and given to Egypt, Jordan and
Israel. Through these old eyes I see
1967, when Israelis decided that the
Egyptian and Jordan sections were their
Holy Land and they occupied land
That we lived on.
We remember being invaded, ordered to move.

Before that, I remember that
Paradise and Heaven were springtime.
Gardens and groves bursting with colors
Vivid greens and pinks. Mostly shades of
Pink from apricot, almond, and tamarisk trees.
We could walk, shop, travel or work
Gather food from our farms. We were
Happy and our children ran and played
Along these roads. The air was filled with
Innocent laughter and greetings.
We could sit outside and see open sky
We lived in peace but now

      The grove is dry dirt.
Missiles bombed flowering groves
      No apricots here

      No water no plants
Children play near raw sewage
      Refugees are trees.

Through these old eyes, I saw us
Forced into relocation camps without
Infrastucture. We are crammed together
On small plots of land, where we are
Forced to build upward
Along narrow streets.
The UN won't help us—

There are villages of shadows woven by
Threads of sunlight. Now when I look
Up, I see patches of sky. During air raids
We run into the darkness of hot,
Small shuttered spaces. If we can't buy food
Before the siren sounds or if bread runs out,
We don't eat. When it rains, sealed rooms
Fill with the stench of death, disease and sewage.
The stench is so thick we can't eat our food.
Every breath burns our stomachs.
I have seen dead Arabs along these roads—
A man, women, children or piles of bodies.

These old eyes have seen their holocaust photos.
So why oppress and torture us?
They have no right to make us suffer.
How fast they forget what Nazis did.
These old eyes have seen compassion in glances
I know, from some of the older ones.
There is nothing but sadistic darkness
In the faces of the new ones transported,
Not born on our land.

At this age now, I pass the time
Playing backgammon with my friend.
When the dice roll from our old
Swollen, weary hands, I remember
We had businesses, took care of families,
Worked our farms when we were young.
Blessed and lucky, now lucky to be alive.
Yes, these old eyes have seen Heaven and Paradise.
Heaven and Paradise were springtime.
Beautiful, blooming days with children's laughter.
I will die in a fine, white and purple robe
Where the land is covered with flowering
Apricot, almond, and olive trees.
Everything will bloom in shades of
Pink and green, the land will be fertile
And the flowerpots and villages
Will not be the skulls or
Tells of Arab people.

Note: A "tell" is a small mound or hill of rubble or ruins that develops as a result of people or
civilizations having settled and been destroyed on that spot of land.

A Poet's Stroke

woman
wrapped
in right side sarcophagus
with small arterial chip
causing

interruption
of gray wave
striation and bone

speaks

wurrrrths   (words
acwosssth   across
sssthiicggh   thick
ssstonggh.   tongue.)

an abstract
liquid
falls
onto
lap.

an immobile
fin
scribbles
universal symbols.

she
is understood.

she
is saved
by a concentric string of words

forced
from
stasis

In the Yard

Depravation comes
Waking lifetimes of struggle—
Endangered species.

Who are blank faces?
Nameless bodies in cycles?
          A stock investment.

Beyond alfalfa
Bee farms' honey, corn and cows
Prisons eat Black men.

Overheard in a subtext of the non-existing disappearing:

Recycled garbage!
Where's accountability?
Who will transform them?

Note: This poem was written on June 28, 2008 at 9:55 a.m. for a Broadside Press Institute of Cultural Studies poetry workshop. It is a response to the *DonDiva Magazine* article, Vol. 8, Issue 92, "Black Men...an Endangered Species."

Yurugu

for Victoria Alexander, baritone saxophonist

Recall the Beginning
Before Africa became a known
Egyptian word / Roman word
Where Dogon call Amma / and becomes the
Cosmos / walking in circles to show
The position of a distant star
Unknown to modern men
Stuck in a science of becoming
Like God—

Recall the Beginning / Space.
Where space is darkness
Lit by ethereal light
Where the Invisible One
Reaches inside Itself to
Create forward motion of
Chaos to Order.

Where Egg is sacred and
Seed is sacred water
Commanding an existence as the
Rhythm of sunlight / moonlight / sunlight
Shattering sound into
Particles of music
The scale / tone / beat of
Sacred ash across bone and marrow
Arranged inside cartography / a map of seas
Capitalist routes with
Black bodies as cargo.

Blown like sacred ash
A sandstorm in a dust bowl rising
To destroy twilight zones of
Systemic madness.

Listen / Listen
Listen to the incantation
The mantra and wail of
Sanity rising from the
Dust of destruction

Listen / Listen
To the Whole Earth purging
Insanity from its psyche / purging
The cynical psychobabble of
Admired Truths turned into
Possessions
Stuffed like silk into a
Tweed breast pocket
Listen / Listen
To the Whole Earth purging
The suffering of souls

Listen / Listen to *this* wind
Turning pain into Beauty
What we hear now
Rising to break
The schism / disunity
Of what was known as Community.

Sound
When sound becomes Jazz and
Jazz is the hands of God
Reaching and ripping
The Blindfold of Ignorance
From the terrain of brain
Matter / the duality of flesh
So the Soul can burst as
Living Water in a
Drum circle's beat
A concentric voice
Talking and whispering
Codes of Truth.

Remember the Beginning
The separated twin / the single birth entity
Once known as a jackal
Mating with placenta to bring forth a mate—
Yurugu / Guardian of Chaos
Projecting the flow of imagination
Imagination spinning in a muddy pool
Found dead in a dream / brought back to life
To bring forth streams
Feeding roots of fragrant flowers

Filling the sky with a mumbling of reeds
Ivory / stretched skin on wood / contained
Inside the timelessness of Creation
Where the bodies of women become
Hummingbirds in flight
The tall walk of flamingoes pink
From living on toxic water—

Listen to this music
The voice of clouds
Weeping healing waters
Evolving into The New
Vocabularies of Culture
Identity / History / Beliefs
Wisdom / Spirit / Art
Epistemologies of Soul
Found in a pot of
Yam-Okra-Rice
Found in wrinkled hands
Along lifelines of scattered bones
Communing with the Ancestors
The Lost / The Living / The Found

Existing in the Levitation of Notes
Pounded by ivory / where horns are pipes
Blowing / the sweat of Freedom
All red plants shrinking
The cancer in the Abandoned / Ostracized
The Outcast / Forsaken / and Forgotten
Bravely facing transition to the Heavens
Where their breath is exhaled as the
Flame of Elemental / First principles of music
Basic unit of harmonics
Contrasting and complementary
Tone tones / Making stones speak
The heat of fusion found in bodies
Illustrated as maps
Humans projected as sinusoidal
Straight lines curving
North and South / Connecting scattered souls
Seen in a vision from
Recalling the Beginning

Yurugu / Recall the Beginning
Yurugu / Recall the Beginning
Blown like sacred ash
(blow)
Blown like sacred ash
(blow)
Blow us into
The Amen / The Source / The Itongo[1]
The Asili of Ani[2]
Her logos of a culture
The seed of culture
Take us to the Utamawazo[3]
The Utamaroho[4]
What makes this music
An energy source / of a culture once
Erased / stolen / hidden
Brought back to the living
Recall the beginning

Yurugu! / Yurugu
I'm calling you!
Yurugu!
Recall the beginning!

Blown like sacred ash

Blown like sacred ash

---

1 Kamitic: States of God before creation. See Kamitic Tree of Life at www.tehutionline.com/newpage.28.htm
2 See *Yurugu: An African-Centered Critique of European Cultural Thought and Behavior* by Marimba Ani (2004). Asili is the logos of a culture. Yurugu is also discussed in *African Myths and Tales* (Feldman, S., 1963, pp. 67-69; Dell Publishers).
3 Utamawazo is culturally structured thought. See ref. # 2 Glossary of *Yurugu* by Marimba Ani (2004)
4 Utamaroho is the vital force of a culture set in motion by the Asili. See ref. # 2 Glossary of *Yurugu* by Marimba Ani (2004).

A Circular Breathing of Sunrise

Selected Parts of Opus 27: A Jazz Poem

For Congressman John Conyers and
the folks at H.R. 57 jazz club in Washington, DC

I

She is walking and inside third set of
Her 54 steps, a long, black Cadillac
Swings around corner blaring
Charles Mingus's *II B.S.* Back inside she
Hits control buttons and searches for Black
Black and white movies never called *Classic*
Till Civil Rights moved freedom into
Affordable RCA consoles pre-cable
Surfing pre-Hip Hop accessibility for
Inner city heads attempting Modern
Urban-izms in Post Modern cubes with
Egg-shaped red fur covered stereo
System swivel chairs chipped from Mod
In front of Avenger Steed / Peel sixties
Judo move shakedowns surfacing in
Backs of heads to crawl frontal lobes
Pickled with boredom.

One hundred cable stations later / she finds
Sidney Poitier with a sax. Sidney
Looking like her daddy
Talkin' 'bout race
In a "Paris Blues" black and white.
Sax in hand and
Leaning against a dresser
He don't be de
Emotional Negro torn between clubbing
And minimalist living. She fingers the red
Wax and takes a swig enough to make
White noise snow gray inside static.

Back to
Piano notes being strings of intermittent
Raindrops / music speeds into full storm.
She sits back and finds life capitulates in
Colors of sound staggered movements
Felt in dawn cracking another day for

Walks in lost realities driven towards
Distant midnights dying.

II

She says: How many people understand
Cecil Taylor's "Nefertiti?"
Wayne Shorter's "El Gaucho?"
Hemispheric distinctions between
Artistic / Imagination / Inspiration
Intuition / creating Metaphoric Self as
Unit?

Poetic music
Phrasing language as *Total* is a blink
Containing fingers moving sequential notes to
Holistic / dye-free paper.

She says:
This is a Cosmic Tit transforming jazz
Theory for the thirsty to suck on.
The Translation of I / We is read in things
Immediately losing complex existence.

She says:
Open is Closed not bound by limits.
Hear it in this as not this. Open is a
Trickle of 4:26 a.m. sensing completion
When the non-existence of time moves
Open to always finding. Who can
Re-mix the nucleus of
Impression
Breath or a
Feeling in a flux of
Un-uttered thoughts
Screaming to be
Improvisation? An unplanned
Sax of un-rehearsed
Impulse?

Take this wax
This sigh this scent and
Spin it inside speakeasy smoke-ring.

Someone grab A-Train / it's going
Somewhere in haute couture / fly / raggin'
Dap-Dan-A-Mug / all duked out / matchin'
Lime Green Gator Daytwah hook up.
She turns and makes her mark sipping straight no
Chaser twilight in sudden hard rain with
Fast breaks breaking a
Memory's eggshell.
She pictures lover's tongue in her mouth
Sliding
Slowly across her soul.
She re-members a
Sliver of pleasure.

III

Somewhere out   there
Someone fights sweet moans growing from
Pulse near inseam pressed against tight skirt.

Somewhere out there
A mind is playing
Body and Soul like a ray of sun
Pleading to be complete fractions
Understood in the shine of
Coltrane's forehead.

IV

a body
vibrates
in a
polarity of
funk.

V

Re-create the mystical blur of rage.
Play an instrument.
Read a book.
Write Poetry as Music.

VI

Where's Max Roach's
"Garvey's Ghost?"
Need to break intimate
Rings of
Numbness.

VII   Commentary

She says:
No. There are no translations.
This conversation is a vibrating wave
Squeezed from a pure realm of
Incomprehensible coherence.
This
Is the genius and beauty of
Jazz. Meditate on
Intuiting the transformation
Of spirit into sound

VIII

Rub and roll this music
Between your fingers.
Stand in front of a mirror and see a
Continent in Coltrane's "Africa," man.
This is truth
Birthed from a blazing hum in
Neon fusion.

IX Waking Vision 2
    July 25, 2006, 6:05 p.m.

Sun burned morning rain clouds into
Bright
Heat wave of
Wasps and
Yellow jackets gliding in
Sunrays to
Wayne Shorter's "Valse Triste."

Nature has her own rituals moving to jazz laid back

We watch / listen / thrash / coil / uncoil
Shrug / and / flail to heal our wounds.
John Coltrane's "India" shakes us loose to
Shake up pain 'til body becomes an orgasmic pulse
Pushing tears to crystallize as drops of
Mind flight cleansing.

Wounds vanish into the cracks of sidewalks
Green, cool grass swallows wounds
Feet stomp as lungs spit dead air

Here
Marrow is fire
The sound of Max Roach's
"Man From South Africa"
Drumming up the foam of death
Escaping to be renewed as a
Rhapsody of living.

Here
Jazz-life obliterates pain
Picks up and moves fast as a
Swarm of ants
Focused on   tomorrow's
Survival.

Note: H.R. 57 is a House of Representatives bill that was introduced by Congressman John Conyers. The bill was passed to preserve jazz as an American art form.